21st Century
Basic Skills
Library

WHAT DO ANIMALS DO IN SPRING?

by Jenna Lee Gleisner

Cherry Lake Publishing • Ann Arbor, Michigan

1

Published in the United States of America
by Cherry Lake Publishing
Ann Arbor, Michigan
www.cherrylakepublishing.com

Consultant: Marla Conn, ReadAbility, Inc.

Photo Credits: Shutterstock Images, Cover, Title, 4, 18; Creative Nature/ Shutterstock Images, 6; Chris Mansfield/iStockphoto, 8; Gregg Williams/ Shutterstock Images, 10; Scott Payne/Shutterstock Images, 12; Cheryl E. Davis/Shutterstock Images, 14; Betty Shelton/Shutterstock Images, 16; Sharon Day/Shutterstock Images, 20

Library of Congress Cataloging-in-Publication Data
Gleisner, Jenna Lee, author.
  What do animals do in spring? / by Jenna Lee Gleisner.
     pages cm. -- (Let's look at spring)
  Audience: 5-7.
  Audience: K to grade 3.
  Includes index.
  ISBN 978-1-62431-660-9 (hardcover) -- ISBN 978-1-62431-687-6 (pbk.) -- ISBN 978-1-62431-714-9 (pdf) -- ISBN 978-1-62431-741-5 (hosted ebook)
 1. Animal behavior--Juvenile literature. 2. Spring--Juvenile literature. I. Title.

  QL751.5.G54 2014
  591.5--dc23
                                                    2013029054

Cherry Lake Publishing would like to acknowledge the work of The Partnership for 21st Century Skills. Please visit www.p21.org for more information.

Printed in the United States of America
Corporate Graphics Inc.
January 2014

TABLE OF CONTENTS

Spring Begins

Spring begins after winter.
Days get warmer.

What Do You See?

What did the mouse find to eat?

Plants grow again. Animals find new food to eat.

Ready for Babies

Animals **mate** to produce babies. Frogs lay their eggs in ponds.

Canada geese **migrate** north. They make nests. Soon they will lay eggs.

A doe finds a safe spot. She will give birth to a fawn.

What Do You See?

How many baby robins do you see?

Babies

Baby robins hatch from eggs.
They are safe in the nest.

Baby animals are born.
A fawn learns to walk.

Bears come out of **hibernation**. Bear cubs play and learn how to find food.

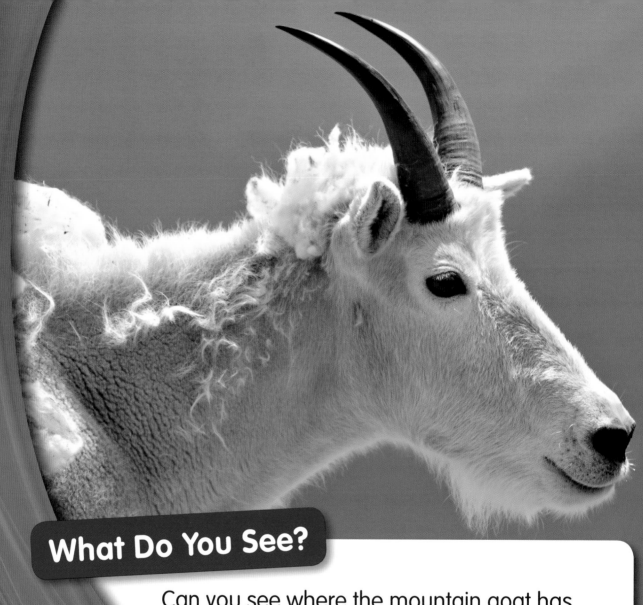

What Do You See?

Can you see where the mountain goat has started to shed its coat?

Spring Ends

The weather warms. Mountain goats **shed** their coats. Summer will be here soon!

Find Out More

BOOK

Rustad, Martha E.H. *Animals in Spring.* Mankato, MN:
  Capstone, 2013.

WEB SITE

Creature Feature—National Geographic Kids
*www.kids.nationalgeographic.com/kids/animals
  /creaturefeature*
Learn facts about all of your favorite animals.

Glossary

hibernation (HYE-bur-nay-shuhn) an animal's sleep that
  lasts all winter long
mate (MATE) to join together to make babies
migrate (MYE-grate) to move from one area to another
shed (SHED) to lose or get rid of

Home and School Connection

Use this list of words from the book to help your child become a better reader. Word games and writing activities can help beginning readers reinforce literacy skills.

animals	eggs	learn	safe
babies	fawn	mate	shed
bears	find	migrate	spot
birth	food	mountain	spring
born	frogs	nests	summer
Canada	geese	north	walk
coats	goats	plants	warmer
cubs	grow	play	weather
days	hatch	ponds	winter
doe	hibernation	produce	
eat	lay	robins	

What Do You See?

What Do You See? is a feature paired with select photos in this book. It encourages young readers to interact with visual images in order to build the ability to integrate content in various media formats.

You can help your child further evaluate photos in this book with additional activities. Look at the images in the book without the What Do You See? feature. Ask your child to point out one detail in each image, such as a color, time of day, animal, or setting.

Index

About the Author

Jenna Lee Gleisner is an editor and author who lives in Minnesota. She loves seeing all of the active animals in spring—especially the frogs in her pond!